ZAC EFRON

Annual 2009

POSY EDWARDS

And In The Beginning Was ... ZAC!

★ FAMILY LIFE

Before dazzling Hollywood with his awesome acting abilities and gorgeous smile, Zac's childhood was idyllic. He spent his early years skateboarding around the sun-kissed Californian streets of his hometown, Arroyo Grande. Neighbours would often see the cheery young lad rolling past their drive on his board, books in arm, on his way to school.

Zac comes from a regular blue-collar family. His parents met at the Arroyo Grande electrical plant, where they both worked in the early eighties. Zac's home life was largely made up of studying for school and messing around with his brother, Dylan, four years Zac's junior. While Zac is the arty performer of the family, Dylan thinks of himself as the athlete, and is seriously into sports. Growing up, Dylan was also always the mischievous one in the Efron household and loved pulling pranks on his big bro. Zac remembers a time when, 'Dylan made me reach into a dark, scary hole to look for a golf ball he "accidentally" threw in. When I put my hand down there, he screamed "SNAAAAAKE!" at the top of his lungs. I almost passed out. He laughed!'

Despite Zac's galactic success, he's still super-close to Dylan, who regularly reminds him he is still young and that he shouldn't get too carried away in the hectic Hollywood whirlwind. According to Zac, their relationship remains very normal. 'As my dad says, I love to stoop to his level. We're just brothers. We goof off and inevitably we fight. We have to fight – it's in our blood.'

> Zac on his hometown, Arroyo Grande: 'It's nice and warm, the perfect town to grow up in.'

With his crazy acting schedule taking up so much of his time, Zac finds it hard to spend quality time with his family, in particular Dylan. 'I wish I could say I spend more time with him,' says Zac. Some of Zac's favourite memories are from when he, his brother and his dad would drive to the San Francisco Giants stadium to watch his sporting heroes play baseball. After the game the three guys would hang around the car park like groupies, waiting to try to get a glimpse of their sporting heroes and possibly grab an autograph or two.

SCHOOL DAYS

Arroyo Grande High, where Zac spent his school days, was your stereotypical all-American high school, with all the cliques and groups that the movies would have you believe in. In fact, according to Zac, it wasn't really that different to *High School Musical*'s East High. Zac reminisces that: 'It was very similar [to East High], only with less spontaneous singing and dancing.'

Because he was so into acting and the performing arts, and was constantly nipping off to Hollywood auditions, Zac was always going to be a little bit of an outsider, so he never fell into any particular gang. Being the laid-back, amiable lad that he is, he had friends all over the place. 'In high school, I really didn't have a clique. I was more of a floater. I tried to hang out with everyone. I had friends in all groups.' From the nerds to the jocks, Zac was everybody's pal, even the teachers'! According to Zac: 'Teachers are people too. Get to know them. Well, don't "suck up", but develop a relationship with each one individually. If you do a good job, the teachers feel morally obliged to give you every possible advantage in their class ... oh, come on! Everyone knows it; I'm just saying it!' Controversial, eh? Zac always does like to say it how it is!

Zac on schoolwork: 'I was always a sort of bookworm. I always tried to get the best grades, and I'm proud of that.'

Despite missing large chunks of term through auditions and acting commitments, Zac always made sure he did his homework on time and never demanded special treatment from his teachers. When Zac graduated in 2006, he obtained a grade point average of 4.3, which is equivalent to an A+ in *every* subject.

BLOSSOMING CAREER

Zac's talent was obvious to his parents from an early age. At three years of age, Zac was obsessed with musicals. He loved the old classics like *The Wizard of Oz* and *The Jungle Book*, and he would always sing along to the words of his favourite songs. By the time Zac turned 11, he was constantly singing some happy tune or another. By this stage, his parents were well aware that he had talent and encouraged him to join the local theatre group. Despite initial butterflies at the audition, Zac landed his first part as the newsboy, and 'from day one I got addicted to being on stage and getting applause and laughter.' Zac never looked back and has been performing ever since.

While still at middle school, Zac continued his theatre work and signed up for drama class, where his teacher insisted on sending him to a talent agent in Hollywood. Of course, his flashing smile and humble charm ensured that he was snapped up straight away. Getting the agent was easy, but landing his first Hollywood job was a little tougher.

Zac's mother would drive him up and down the freeway from Arroyo Grande to Los Angeles up to three times a week in the hope of landing his first gig. Rejection followed rejection as Zac soon learned that Hollywood was a tough place to make a living. Despite this he embraced a positive attitude and refused to let it get him down. 'You have to do your best every time, but after each audition you have to forget about it. You always have to be looking forward and not look back.'

Zac's mature and positive attitude held him in good stead and he soon landed his first TV role. He got the role of Simon (also the name of his Siamese cat) in an episode of *Firefly*, a futuristic sci-fi show for Fox. Soon enough, Zac was popping up in well-known TV shows such as *ER* and *CSI Miami*. Having completed his first TV movie with Aidan Quinn and Mary Louise-Parker – for which he received a Young Artists Awards nomination – people in the industry began to take note of the talented young teenager. Soon his big break would come …

SUMMERLAND DAYS

Zac became an overnight heart-throb in the US when he played the guest role of Cameron Bale, a soulful and mysterious surfer, in the hit TV show *Summerland*. Originally only scripted in for two episodes, the producers and audience loved him so much that the role was extended. Soon enough, TV audiences were getting the chance to swoon over Zac wearing not much more than a pair of boardies while he strutted around the beach for the cameras. Unfortunately, Zac soon found that good things always come to an end, and often very abruptly. Despite the show's and Zac's success, *Summerland* was cancelled by head office. Zac learned the hard way that nothing is permanent in showbiz.

Zac on his *Summerland* character, Cameron Bale:
'It was all about the drama. My character has some really deep and heavy issues. Luckily, I've never had to deal with the kind of intense pain he's had to deal with. That makes it really exciting for me.'

BIG SCREEN BREAK

Despite the setback of having his television big break cancelled, Zac's career continued to rocket towards the stars. It wasn't long before movie execs began to sit up and take notice of the boy enigma who was dazzling the screen every time he performed. *The Derby Stallion* was Zac's first big-screen production. However, before filming began, Zac found out that there was a catch to the equestrian-based movie. 'I'd never done any horseback riding. I assumed when I signed on for this movie that it was all going to be done by stuntmen. Then the first day when I came on set and talked to one of the producers, he said, "Yes, you have three lessons and you're going to be jumping!" I guess that really turned on my adrenaline.' Ever the pro, Zac picked it up in no time and, as a result, he still loves horses to this day.

> **Zac on his love of horse riding:** 'It's a different experience and, at the same time, it's fun! It's so thrilling and amazing to be on top of a horse.'

THE MAKING OF HIGH SCHOOL MUSICAL

One quiet morning, Zac got a call from his agent telling him that he had the perfect project for him, but that it was about to start filming and it was the last day of auditions. The film was called *High School Musical*. Zac had never heard of it, but jumped in the car with his mum and drove down the highway to Los Angeles while his agent frantically made arrangements to get Zac into the auditions.

It was the last day of their long search for talent and the Disney producers were frustrated at not having found the perfect guy to play the lead role of heart-throb Troy Bolton. Just before they were about to pack up and go home, cool as ever, Zac strutted through the audition room doors and blew them all away with his sparkling blue eyes and handsome grin. *High School Musical* had found their leading star.

The rehearsals and shooting of *HSM* were pretty tough for the young and relatively inexperienced cast. Zac says: 'We didn't know what we were doing; we were thrown into this dance room and there were mirrors everywhere! We didn't know anything about each other and had to learn these dances. We had two weeks of intense dancing, acting, singing and basketball rehearsals, along with strange stretching exercises and things I'd never heard of before. We'd wake up at six in the morning and work until six at night. I learned more in those two weeks than I'd learned in all the previous years.'

By the time it came to filming, Zac and the rest of the cast did a stellar job and everyone was confident that they'd made something special. However, no one could have guessed at the phenomenal success that was to come.

HIGH SCHOOL MUSICAL MANIA

On the first screening, *HSM* pulled in 7.7 million viewers, smashing all of Disney's records. Zac claims the major reason for the success of *HSM* is the fact that it has a little something for everyone: 'Girls love the romance and boys love the whole basketball and sports angle of the show.' After *HSM*, his world would never be the same again. Due to its amazing reception, Disney aired the film 11 more times. In a matter of weeks, Zac and the gang had reached 36 million viewers worldwide – and every one of them became an overnight Zac fanatic.

The following years saw *High School Musical 2* and *3* come out, and Zac's popularity went through the stratosphere. Summer 2007 became known as 'The Summer of Zac' and the boy wonder became the hottest thing in Tinseltown since Leonardo DiCaprio.

BIG TIME

Zac's arrival on the Hollywood hot-list saw plenty of big money offers come pouring in. But, ever the entertainer, Zac wanted to stay true to his song-and-dance roots, so he went for the part of Link Larkin in the remake of the eighties classic, *Hairspray*. In the musical he got to play opposite Hollywood heavyweights such as Christopher Walken and Queen Latifah.

But Zac was really blown away by working with his idol, John Travolta, who played the role of Tracy Turnblad's mother. Many have compared the two, saying that the all-singing, all-dancing kid is the Travolta of our time. Certainly, Zac's performance as Link Larkin is the coolest display of sixties slickness since Danny Zuko raced Thunder Road in *Grease*. In fact, in June 2008 he won the Best Breakthrough Performance award for his role at the MTV Movie awards. One of Zac's favourite parts of working with his hero was catching private renditions of the *Grease* songs: 'Very few people get to see John perform those songs in person, but we got to see him do it dressed as a woman. It was a privilege.'

The 2008 release of *Seventeen Again* saw Zac play the teenage version of *Friends* star Matthew Perry. In it Zac plays the role of the teenage Mike O'Donnell, who as an adult – played by Matthew Perry – gets the chance to be a kid again and change his life. The film is Zac's first lead in a rom-com, and if the success of last summer's movie is anything to go by, we can expect plenty more in the future.

THE ZAC QUIZ

Think you know **everything** there is to know about our **Hollywood hunk**? Take the Zac quiz and see how many points you score to find out if you're Zac's biggest know-it-all fan.

1. What are Zac's two middle names?

a) James and Peter
b) Mark and Steven
c) David and Alexander
d) Jonny and Martin

2. What is Zac's star sign?

a) Aquarius
b) Libra
c) Aries
d) Scorpio

3. What TV show did Zac star in with his first crush, Lori Laughlin?

a) *Baywatch*
b) *Full House*
c) *Summerland*
d) *The OC*

4. What is Zac's brother's name?

a) Bob
b) Dylan
c) Elton
d) John

5. Who is his favourite musician?

a) Justin Timberlake
b) Kanye West
c) Usher
d) John Mayer

6. In which Californian town was Zac born?

a) Los Angeles
b) San Francisco
c) San Luis Obispo
d) Monterey

7. What is Zac's favourite animal?

a) Lion
b) Tiger
c) Liger (the lion and tiger mix-breed)
d) Dog

8. What is Zac's favourite movie?

a) *Goonies*
b) *Star Wars*
c) *Shrek*
d) *High School Musical*

9. Who does Zac consider his greatest role model to be?

a) John Travolta
b) Peter Parker
c) Clark Kent
d) Leonardo DiCaprio

10. What is Zac's nickname amongst his school pals?

a) Hollywood
b) Ziggy
c) Pretty Boy
d) Z Man

11. What is Zac's Siamese cat called?

a) Tiger
b) Bangles
c) Chris
d) Simon

12. What is Zac's favourite cartoon?

a) *Ben 10*
b) *Alvin and the Chipmunks*
c) *Sponge Bob Square Pants*
d) *Rocco's Modern Life*

13. What is Zac's favourite take-away food?

a) Chinese
b) Pizza
c) Sushi
d) Mexican

14. What is Zac's dream car?

a) Toyota Supra
b) Volkswagen Beetle
c) Lamborghini
d) Ferrari

15. What is Zac's worst habit?

a) Picking his nose
b) Humming
c) Talking with his mouth full
d) Whistling

16. If Zac could have any sports celebrity's autograph, whose would it be?

a) David Beckham
b) Shaquille O'Neal
c) Kobe Bryant
d) Eli Manning

17. What movie anthem does Zac have as his ringtone?

a) *Rocky*
b) *Star Wars*
c) *Ghostbusters*
d) *Top Gun*

18. Which actress is Zac's dream woman?

a) Lindsay Lohan
b) Jessica Alba
c) Angelina Jolie
d) Penelope Cruz

19. What is Zac's favourite city?

a) New York
b) Sydney
c) Tokyo
d) London

20. What can't Zac start the day without?

a) A bowl of cereal
b) A good sing in the shower
c) A run
d) A swim

How many did you score? Add up your points to see how much of a Zac know-it-all you are.

16-20 – You know more about Zac than he knows about himself. You're his number one Zactastic fan!

11-15 – Wow you really know your stuff, you're a top fan.

6-10 – You know your Zac facts, but not enough. You're a could-do-better fan.

0-5 – You need to get swatting up on your Zac knowledge. You're only a half-hearted fan.

Test your friends and see who knows Zac the best. (Answers on page 61)

Make Your Own ZAC BADGE

Show your friends that you love Zac the most with your very own homemade Zac badges

YOU WILL NEED:

♥ Lots of different pictures of Zac cut out from magazines

♥ Old badges

♥ Scissors

♥ Glue

♥ Coloured pens

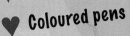

INSTRUCTIONS:

1. Choose a badge that's a similar size to Zac's face in one of your pictures.

2. Place the badge over the picture of Zac's face and use your scissors to cut out the picture of Zac around the badge.

3. Using your glue, stick a picture of Zac to the badge.

4. With a colourful pen write things like I ♥ Zac, or your name and Zac's on the badge.

5. If you wanted, you could stick your picture on the badge next to Zac's face – don't let Vanessa see it, though!

Full name: Zachary David Alexander Efron

Nickname: Hollywood

Birthdate: 18 October 1987

Sign: Libra

Hometown: Arroyo Grande, San Luis Obispo, California

Height: 5'9"

Parents: David and Starla

Siblings: Dylan, 14

Pets: Two Australian Shepherds, Dreamer and Puppy, and a Siamese cat, Simon

About his pets: 'My dogs are crazy. They're always getting into some kind of trouble ... but then again, they're my most loyal friends'

Favourite foods: Orange chicken from Panda Express, sushi, Wheat Thins, Japanese and exotic foods

Favourite cereals: Kashi, granola, Honey Nut Cheerios and Quaker Oats

Heaven on earth is: 'Being first in line when the "Krispy Kreme" employees hand out the free samples'

For dinner, Zac likes to make: 'Mac n Cheese! All the other stuff is too hard!'

His most prized possession: His autographed baseball collection. 'I've got almost every player from the Giants for the past ten years'

First financial splurge: 'I bought an electric scooter in sixth grade. It bankrupted me'

Before I die, I want to: 'Discover I really do have super powers ... I just didn't know it yet!'

People would be surprised that I: 'Am just like they are'

Magazines Zac subscribes to: M&F, GQ, Cargo and Popstar! 'Only because they have good posters of Jesse [McCartney] ... Joke, dude!'

Boxers or briefs: Both!

Favourite TV show: Most Extreme Elimination Challenge, American Idol and The Wiggles

ZAC FACTS

Favourite actor/actress: Way too many to answer ...

Favourite musician/band: Right now? ... Postal Service

Favourite movie: The Goonies, 'hands down!'

Favourite music: Anything but country!

Favourite cartoon: Rocko's Modern Life

Favourite TV channel: Spike

Favourite book: Robinson Crusoe by Daniel Defoe

Favourite animal: Ligers (the lion and tiger mix-breed)

Favourite guilty pleasure: Comic books and video games

Favourite quote: 'I'll be back' from Terminator II

Role model: Peter Parker

Biggest fear: Zombies, sharks and the girl from The Ring

Ticklish? Yes!

Allergies? None!

His hidden talent: 'I can blow bubbles with my spit'

Weirdest dream: 'I'm underwater and I can breathe and talk to fish and stuff. It was crazy'

On doing dares: 'I'll eat just about anything – like blending up steak and apples, and then drinking it'

On his driving test: 'I cracked a cheesy joke and the instructor didn't laugh at all!'

Dream car: Toyota Supra from The Fast and the Furious

When I fly I have to have: 'Rocket boots! Otherwise I always seem to fall'

What I'm reading: Naruto, Volume 7

The DVD release he was most excited about: Lords of Dogtown

17

HIGH SCHOOL MUSICAL

For Zac, playing the cool-as-ice part of Troy Bolton is a dream role and, wow, does he certainly have the good looks, charisma and talent to light up the screen each time he performs. But he couldn't have done it without the stellar back-up of Hollywood's brightest young stars.

> Zac on doing *High School Musical* 2 and 3: 'It was great to be with all the guys again. It was fun. Like a reunion.'

★ THE CAST

Vanessa Hudgens

Just like Zac, this leading lady started her career in her local theatre. Her exotic looks and enchanting voice made sure she was quickly snapped up by Hollywood talent agents. Aged just 15, she starred in her first movie, *Thirteen*. She then went on to forge ties with the folk at Disney when she worked on *Thunderbirds*. Just like Zac, she guest starred in *The Suite Life of Zack and Cody* alongside Ashley Tisdale, with whom she went on to become best friends. Despite all this experience, she was still one of the least-known leading cast members of *HSM*.

Sure enough, the world soon got to know the face and voice of Vanessa Hudgens once *HSM* was aired. The lead actress was the envy of the female world when it was revealed that her and Zac were an item, and 'Zanessa' became the hottest couple since 'Brangelina'.

VANESSA TELLS US ABOUT...

Working with her BFF: 'My best friend is actually Ashley Tisdale! I originally met her on a commercial we did for Sears. After we knew we had gotten *High School Musical* we just ran up and jumped up and down like a pair of little girls. We were so excited!'

Chocolate: 'You give me any kind of chocolate, I will eat it. I've always loved it ever since I was little. I even have it by my bedside.'

Boys: 'I like cute, funny, sweet guys; loyal and honest. I like guys with long hair, but not too long.' Remind you of anyone?

Since the *HSM* phenomenon, Vanessa has become the high school girly icon for every teenager in the world. In 2007, she was signed up by Hollywood Records and released her debut album, and 2009 sees her first lead in a feature film with *Will*, a movie based on the fortunes of a High School rock band.

VANESSA FACTS

- Vanessa can't whistle.

- She keeps a secret diary under her bed.

- Vanessa's guilty pleasures are chocolate and cheeseburgers.

- Her favourite pastime is shopping.

- When relaxing, she loves to curl up on the sofa and watch *Sponge Bob Square Pants*.

Corbin Bleu

- At the *HSM* auditions, Corbin initially tried out for the role of Ryan.

- In his school days, his classmates nominated him the teacher's pet.

- Corbin collects belts. His favourite has his nickname 'Bleuman' written on it.

- Corbin's favourite actor is Johnny Depp.

- He hates mess and stores all his books and CDs in alphabetical order.

The most experienced of all the *HSM* crew, Corbin has been in front of the cameras for the majority of his life, ever since appearing in GAP commercials as a cute baby. His sweet, boyish looks and awesome dancing skills meant that he sailed through the *HSM* auditions with ease, and was the perfect guy to play the role of Troy's best friend, Chad Danforth. He's also got a budding singing career and his album, *Another Side*, was released in 2007.

CORBIN TELLS US ABOUT...

Chad: 'Chad is a very passionate person about everything he does, which is something we have in common. Where we are not alike is that Chad is not open to new things. I love change.'

Performing: 'I get so nervous I can't sing. I freak out when I hear my own voice.'

Himself: 'I am secure with who I am. I march to the beat of my own drum.'

Fun in the sun: 'I'm a beach person. I love the water! I swear I'm a fish.'

Ashley Tisdale

Certainly the most well-known face before *HSM* started shooting, the blonde bombshell made her name playing the role of Maddie in *The Suite Life of Zack and Cody*. She's also guest-starred in *Beverly Hills 90210*, *Charmed* and the hit flick, *Donnie Darko*. She released her first solo album in 2008 to a massive reception, selling almost a million copies worldwide.

Being best friends with both Zac and Vanessa, she's the glue that makes 'Zanessa' stick together.

ASHLEY TELLS US ABOUT...

Her dream boy: 'I think Jake Gyllenhaal is so cute. If I ever talked to him, I'd end up giggling!'

Sharpay: 'Sharpay is the queen bee. But all of a sudden, things are changing and people are coming out of the cliques, so she's threatened.'

Working for success: 'My parents told me to follow my dreams and to never give up, no matter what happens or if things get hard. It is hard work, so just keep focused and never give up.'

ASHLEY FACTS

- She got the inspiration to play Sharpay from watching Rachel McAdams in the flick *Mean Girls*.

- When she was just twelve years old, she sang at the White House.

- Her favourite film is *My Best Friend's Wedding*.

- Her family nickname is Pookernuts.

- Ashley is the first-ever female artist to have two singles debut at the same time in the US top 100 chart.

Lucas Grabeel

Ryan: 'I'm like Ryan because I have a strong background in theatre and I did a lot of performing while growing up.'

Realising your dreams: 'If it can be dreamed, it can be reached.'

Himself: 'I am a simple, plain person. You know? I'm chilled and laid-back and not so out there and crazy.'

His dream role: 'I'd like to play Kurt Cobain because I want [to portray] someone who has mysteries.'

The HSM audition: 'It was a lot like a theatrical audition. I went in there and did my thing. A month later, I found out I was cast.'

Fame: 'Everywhere I go now, someone says something. At the movie theatre, at the bank, pretty much any public place that kids could be. It's a big deal for them.'

Lucas moved to the bright lights of Hollywood from Springfield, Missouri, with nothing but a few changes of clothes and a head full of dreams. Having sent his headshots and details around the industry's talent scouts, Lucas waited by the phone for a good few weeks in expectation of a response. None came. By pure luck, Lucas bumped into an agent while queuing for a smoothie in an LA mall. The agent snapped him up and later ensured he got in front of the *HSM* casting couch, where he was offered the role of Ryan, and the rest, as they say, is history. 2008 has been a super-busy year for Lucas. He's made three films and in the most notable flick, *Milk*, he works with Hollywood stalwarts Gus Van Sant and Sean Penn.

Lucas Facts

- When he arrived in Hollywood, Lucas worked in a video store to support his budding acting career.

- He loves the old Disney classic *The Fox and the Hound*.

- Lucas is a keen musician, playing both the drums and the guitar.

- A favourite golden-oldie film of Lucas's is *Singin' in the Rain*.

- Lucas has a Maltese poodle called Lilly.

Monique Coleman

One of the older members of the cast, Monique, who plays Taylor McKessie, has done quite a bit of TV work over the years. Like Zac, Vanessa and Ashley, she starred in the *The Suite Life of Zack and Cody*. She's also been in hit shows such as *Malcolm in the Middle*, *Gilmore Girls*, *Boston Public* and *Veronica Mars*. A major goal of hers – which she's certainly achieved – is to be a source of inspiration to others.

MONIQUE FACTS

- Her favourite outdoor activity is camping.

- She is seven years older than Zac.

- Monique's favourite band is the Black Eyed Peas.

- If she had to quit acting she'd like to work in alternative medicine.

MONIQUE TELLS US ABOUT...

Her fellow *HSM* stars: 'We are like family and I really get along with everyone. We see a lot of one another.'

Taylor: 'My character is a little bit brighter in the math and science department than I am – okay, a lot!'

Her favourite musical: '*Fame* is the movie that made me want to be an actress. When I saw *Fame* I said, "I do not just want to be a spectator, but to be a part of it"'!

HIGH SCHOOL MUSICAL 3 Senior Year

Packed with amazing music and a storyline to knock the socks off all Zac fans, *HSM 3: Senior Year* delivers great entertainment to movie goers across the world. But what do the guys get up to in their final year? A lot, is the answer!

Graduating from high school, the Wildcats and all the gang from East High face being separated and going their different ways, but how will our heroes move on? Will Chad achieve his dream of playing college basketball? Will Sharpay and Ryan have glittering careers on the stage?

And most importantly, will Troy and Gabriella stay together? *High School Musical 3* answers all of our questions and more.

And one thing's for sure, no matter what the future holds, the gang know that they'll always have each other.

THE PROM

For any high school senior, nothing is more important than the prom. It's a chance to have one final party with all your friends before everyone moves onwards and upwards. Not only is it pick-your-perfect-date time, you've also got to decide what to wear and how to get there. What type of dress should you choose, and what colour? How are you going to style your hair? Gabriella, Sharpay and Monique are definitely going to be busy bees and Troy, Ryan and Chad have a lot to prepare in order to impress their special ladies.

Well, we all know who our perfect date would be: Zac! But what about that dress? If money was no option, if parents had no say whatsoever, what would you wear to impress Mr Efron? Here's your chance to design the PERFECT prom dress to match that perfect boy on your arm ...

DESIGN YOUR OWN PROM DRESS

Finally, your dream has come true and Zac has asked you to go to the prom – you are one lucky girl! But you'd better get planning right away because the big question is, what on earth will you wear? Here, let your imagination run wild and create your own red carpet gown for this very special night.

YOU WILL NEED:

* Pencil
* Coloured pens
* Scissors
* Sheets of various coloured paper – if you don't have coloured paper use white paper then colour it different shades
* Glitter
* Tinfoil
* Glue

INSTRUCTIONS:

1. First, you must decide on your hair and make-up. Use the pens to colour in the face and hair, deciding if you want to go blonde or brunette, long or short. What colour make-up would you prefer, and what about blusher and lipstick? Remember not to overdo it as Zac likes his girls to look natural.

2. Now for the dress. Decide what colour you'd like and, using a sheet of coloured paper, design the outline of your perfect dress: what about a long skirt or a full princess skirt? Maybe you'd like to wear a short dress with a slanted hem? Keep designing until you are happy, then cut around the shape you have drawn and stick it down onto the mannequin. And now the fun part, if you want a sparkly dress, apply glue to the trim or centre of the dress and sprinkle on a little glitter.

3. Using a pencil or tinfoil – you can roll the tinfoil into small balls – design your earrings, necklaces and rings. When deciding, think about what Vanessa wears. She normally goes for a bracelet, a simple necklace and pretty gold earrings.

4. You may want to try a corsage on your wrist. Zac would usually bring this, but give it a try and see what colour flowers would look great with the dress by drawing them onto the mannequin.

HEY, NOW YOU ARE READY TO PARTY!
HAVE A GREAT TIME WITH YOUR DREAM DATE!

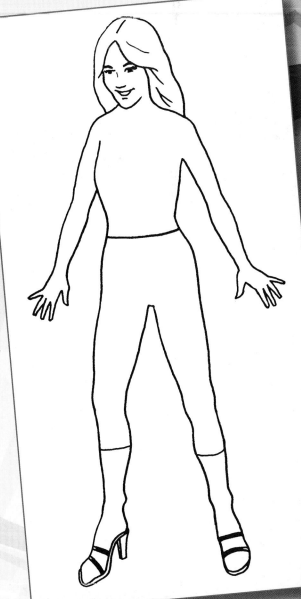

WHICH HIGH SCHOOL MUSICAL STAR ARE YOU?

Take our **personality test** to find out which star you're most like ...

1. You're out to the movies on a hot date. Which film would you most like to see?

a) *Batman Begins*
b) *The Nightmare Before Christmas*
c) *My Best Friend's Wedding*
d) *Chicago*
e) *Moulin Rouge*
f) *Fame*

2. After the movie you go for a bite to eat. What would be your meal of choice?

a) Sushi
b) Chinese
c) McDonalds
d) Anything with French fries
e) Pizza
f) It doesn't matter as long as it's healthy

3. Which of the following artists gets the most airtime on your iPod?

a) John Mayer
b) Hilary Duff
c) Billy Joel
d) Justin Timberlake
e) Nirvana
f) Beyoncé

4. The weekend comes and you're feeling like hitting the outdoors. What's your idea of fun?

a) Surfing
b) Shopping
c) Walking my dog
d) Basketball
e) No outdoors for me, thanks!
f) Camping

5. Which of the following is your greatest celebrity idol?

a) John Travolta
b) Natalie Wood
c) Brittany Murphy
d) Johnny Depp
e) Kurt Cobain
f) Lisa 'Left Eye' Lopes

6. What do you think the key to stardom is?

a) Hard work, dedication and a cool hairstyle
b) Talent and good looks
c) Always looking your best – you never know when you might get discovered!
d) Family connections and standing out from the crowd
e) Self-belief and a bit of luck
f) Work hard, don't just rely on natural talent

7. Which motto best suits your attitude towards school?

a) Form a good relationship with your teachers in order to get the best possible advantage from class

b) Keep your head down, do all your homework and never misbehave

c) Stay true to yourself. Don't follow the crowd

d) Do what's necessary in class to allow you to follow your extra-curricular dreams like basketball and acting

e) It's OK to be different. Don't let anyone hold you back and go for what you want 110%

f) Hard work is the key and always pays off in the end

8. After school do you ...

a) Shoot some hoops then chill out with your boyfriend/ girlfriend

b) Go shopping then hang out with your boyfriend/girlfriend

c) Go straight to singing lessons then bowling with your friends

d) Head straight to basketball practice and play until the sun comes down

e) Go to dance practice then head to the mall to buy the latest trendy threads

f) Go straight home and do your homework before calling your best friend for a gossip

9. What do you look for in a potential boyfriend/ girlfriend?

a) A curvy figure and integrity

b) Honesty and good hair

c) Nice eyes and popularity

d) Athletic physique and good dance moves

e) Good fashion sense and a laid-back personality

f) Outdoorsy personality and an independent nature

10. What's your guilty pleasure?

a) Singing in the shower

b) Chocolate

c) Dying your hair blonde

d) Sausage and pepper sandwiches

e) Accessory shopping

f) Golden-oldie music like Al Green and Barry White

So, how did you get on? Find out by counting up which letter you answered the most. If you scored mostly ...

A's then you've got all the good looks and grace of **Zac Efron**.

B's then you've got the elegance and beauty of **Vanessa Hudgens**.

C's then you've got all the stunning qualities of **Ashley Tisdale**.

D's then you've got the whacky charm of **Corbin Bleau**.

E's then you possess the flashing brilliance of **Lucas Grabeel**.

F's then you've got all the wit and humility of **Monique Coleman**.

Form your own ZAC FAN CLUB

Starting a fan club is a fab way of meeting and getting to know other Zac fans out there. It's also great for sharing info, tips and gossip about Zac.

Where?

First you need to decide where you're going to have your club. You could have weekly meetings at your house or perhaps in your classroom at breaktime. Alternatively you could set up a MySpace, Bebo or Facebook page dedictated to Zac. By going online you could meet fellow Zac fans from around the world. But remember, when online never give out your personal details, and if in doubt, speak to your parents!

When?

You then have to decide how often you're going to hold meetings. You could do a weekly get-together with all your Zac pals, or if you're super keen you could do it daily. Saturday afternoons are always a good time as no one has school. If you're online, you could arrange time for Instant Messenger chats with all your new Zacaholic pals.

Activities

Now that your group is all set up, you'll need some stuff to do. The activities in this book would be a good place to start. You can all do the Zac quiz (on pages 14–15) and see who has the highest score. Or see who can make the prettiest Valentine's Day card or design the fanciest prom dress.

Club meetings or online forums are a good way of sharing and catching up on all the latest Zac goss. You can also show off and share your latest posters. But the best thing to do in a Zac fan club is to collect all the Zac DVDs and gather all your friends together for a sleepover to watch a Zac movie marathon.

Zac Discussion Topics

At your meetings, or if you've set up a Zac fan club page on a social networking site, it's really fun to start some discussions to find out what other fans think of Zac. Fill in your answers here and find out what other people in your fan club think about these hot Zac topics.

Tick off the movies you've got on the Zac filmography below. Have you watched all the Zac flicks at your fan club?

- [ ] *High School Musical 1*
- [ ] *High School Musical 2*
- [ ] *High School Musical 3*
- [ ] *Hairspray*
- [ ] *The Derby Stallion*
- [ ] *Seventeen Again*

OT TOPICS

- [ ] What is Zac's best film?
- [ ] Who should Zac work with in the future?
- [ ] Should Zac release a solo album?
- [ ] What is Zac's best hairstyle?
- [ ] What should Zac get Vanessa for Christmas?
- [ ] What is your favourite Zac song from HSM?

- [ ] Should there be HSM 4?
- [ ] Should Zac and Vanessa get married?
- [ ] If not, who should he marry?
- [ ] Will Zac win an Oscar in the future?

LOVE LIFE

★ YOUNG LOVE

Zac's piercing blue eyes have sent the girls swooning ever since his first day at school, so he was never short of attention even in those awkward early school years. But he never let it distract him from his studies or his acting. Zac always felt that his grades and his career should come before girls. That didn't stop him getting all the attention though! Zac recalls that: 'When I was in first grade, this girl passed me a note in class that said, "Do you like me?" and there was a box that said "check yes or check no." I checked yes and handed it back to her. It was really funny, romantic awesomeness.'

> Zac on forgetting the name of his first kiss, aged 13: 'It was in a game of truth or dare. I can picture her face exactly! I can't believe I can't think of her name.'

WHAT ZAC LOOKS FOR IN A GIRL

How many boxes out of Zac's top ten criteria do you tick?

To be one of Zac's girls, it helps if ...

♡ You have brown hair. While Zac loves a bubbly blonde, his real soft spot is for brunettes.

♡ You've got a good singing voice. Zac loves to sing when pottering around the house, and likes to have a girl he can duet with.

♡ You possess a generous heart. Zac can't stand mean-spirited people, and loves kind folk, like him.

♡ You look curvy. Nothing is less attractive to Zac than skinny, size zero models. 'I like my girls like I like my peanut butter – chunky.'

♡ You smell sweet. Zac loves nothing more on a girl than the smell of 'a good perfume. I like the smell of Pink Sugar.'

♡ You like Japanese food, as he loves going for sushi on dates.

♡ You like to talk. 'I think if a girl is easy to talk to then that's the first thing I look for,' says Zac. 'It's great when you meet a girl and three hours later you're like, "Oh my gosh, we've been talking for three hours, what happened to the time?" I just think that is a great connection and you know there is potential there.'

♡ You have soulful eyes (preferably brown). Zac is a sensitive guy and needs to be able to look deep into a girl's eyes.

♡ You don't get jealous. Zac sees jealousy as a weak personality trait, and will often have to work with other pretty girls, so he needs his girlfriend to trust him.

But watch out!...

♡ Don't hum. It's one of Zac's greatest pet peeves. Zac's worst-ever date was with a girl who hummed. According to Zac, it was 'so annoying'.

EX-GIRLFRIENDS

Ever the mature type, Zac believes in staying friends with his old flames and doesn't like to lose touch with those that have been close to his heart. 'My first crush and I are still friends to this day. We text message and call each other all the time.'

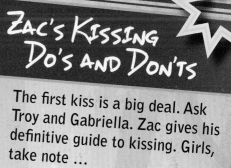

ZAC'S KISSING DO'S AND DON'TS

The first kiss is a big deal. Ask Troy and Gabriella. Zac gives his definitive guide to kissing. Girls, take note …

DO 'Go easy and take your time. Be respectful of the other person and don't just get on in there and grope all over the place. My favourite kisses happen when I've taken it nice and slow.'

DON'T 'Try to swallow the person you're kissing by opening your mouth so wide! I've never experienced a washing machine kiss, but I've heard about them. When girls rotate their tongues around your mouth like a washing machine, that's not a good idea.'

ZANESSA

On the day Zac got the call from his agent telling him to rush down to Hollywood for the final day of *HSM* auditions, two massively important things happened to him. Not only did he try out for the role that would revolutionise his career, but he met the love of his life.

As soon as Zac was introduced to Vanessa, it was love at first sight. The casting directors and everyone else in the auditioning hall could see the sparks flying and they were paired together straight away. Zac reckons that being with Vanessa was a massive bonus. 'We were paired together from the beginning. To some degree, I think that helped us out because we really got to know each other.'

So from day one they've relied on each other, both on and off the screen, and this mutual bond has blossomed into one of Hollywood's greatest love stories. The two have now done three films together and still can't get enough of each other. In their limited spare time, they regularly take romantic road trips up the Californian coast or holidays to Hawaii. Now, as they pursue their independent careers, they'll need each other's off-screen support more than ever.

Ten Reasons Why Zanessa Are Destined To Be Together

Zac and Vanessa's many similarities:

- They're both from California.

- They both started acting as children and were teen stars who liked to act, sing and dance.

- Before *HSM*, the two independently guest-starred on *The Suite Life of Zack and Cody* with Ashley Tisdale, whom they both consider to be one of their closest friends.

- The dream couple are both desperate to go skydiving one day.

- In their most recent films before *High School Musical 3*, they both worked with *Friends* stars. Zac co-starred alongside Matthew Perry, and Vanessa with Lisa Kudrow.

- They love kangaroos.

- *Peter Pan* is one of their favourite children's stories.

- They both hate smoking.

- They're both gorgeous!

Make Your Own
ZAC VALENTINE'S CARD

So, you want to make Zac's heart flutter this Valentine's Day? Create the most romantic card to turn him weak at the knees.

YOU WILL NEED:

* Two pieces of card or paper, coloured or plain
* Glue
* Scissors
* Pens, pencils or paint
* A picture of Zac cut out from a magazine, about 10cm x 10cm
* Sheet of glitter paper

INSTRUCTIONS:

1. Fold one of the pieces of paper in half.

2. From the folded side, cut out a half-heart shape into the paper. Open out the folded piece and you should now have a symmetrical shaped heart.

3. Fold the picture of Zac in half, and cut a smaller half-heart shape from the folded side as before.

4. Stick the heart-shaped picture of Zac to the heart-shaped card or paper.

5. Fold the second piece of card or paper in half. Stick the heart-shaped picture of Zac to the card.

6. Now fold the edge of the glitter paper in by 2cm and cut six half-heart shapes out of the vertically folded strip. Do this four or five times until you have around 25 or so hearts.

7. Put the glitter hearts inside the card, so when Zac opens the card the hearts will sprinkle onto his lap.

If you like, you can write a poem inside ...

Roses are red,
Violets are blue,
But most of all, Zac,
I love you
x x x

AND SEND YOUR CARD TO ZAC AT:

Zac Efron
P.O. Box 960
Avila Beach
CA 93424

Dress Your Own ZAC

Zac certainly wears smokin' threads, but do you think you could do a better job than the smoothest dresser in Hollywood? Why not dress up your own Zac and see ...

YOU WILL NEED:

* Glue
* Coloured pens
* Scissors
* Sheets of various coloured paper (make sure you have green; one of Zac's favourite colours). If you don't have coloured paper use white and colour it in

INSTRUCTIONS:

Cut out lots of different clothes from the pieces of paper (e.g. shirts, T-shirts, jumpers, shorts and trousers) and colour them in according to the style you choose. Stick them to the different Zac mannequins.

SUMMER ZAC

In the summertime, Zac likes to wear baggy shorts and bright coloured T-shirts. Summer Zac loves greens, reds and pale blues (to match his eyes).

SPORTY ZAC

A bright red Wildcat tracksuit is what Zac likes to wear when he's working out. Cut out some red bottoms and a top and draw in the Wildcats symbol on the chest.

GO WILDCATS

Surfer Zac

Zac loves bright, flowery Hawaiian-style board shorts when he's ripping up the waves. Cut out a pair of knee-length shorts and colour them in with bright, pretty flowers.

Winter Zac

In the colder months, Zac likes to go for more neutral colours. Maybe try a brown, grey or black V-neck jumper with a pair of slim-fitting navy jeans.

ZAC'S BIRTHDAY QUIZ

Do you know enough about Zac to spend time with him on his birthday? Take the Zac birthday challenge to find out ...

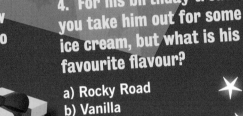

1. First you'll need to know when the special day is, so when is Zac's birthday?

a) 19 October
b) 18 October
c) 18 November
d) 19 November

2. For Zac's birthday breakfast-in-bed, what would he prefer to eat?

a) Granola
b) Bacon and eggs
c) Cornflakes
d) Yoghurt

3. For his first present you download Zac an album, but which band would he prefer?

a) Arctic Monkeys
b) The Killers
c) Postal Service
d) Foo Fighters

4. For his birthday treat you take him out for some ice cream, but what is his favourite flavour?

a) Rocky Road
b) Vanilla
c) Cherry Garcia
d) Chocolate

5. Zac loves adrenaline sports, so what would be his activity of choice on his special day?

a) Skydiving
b) Bungee jumping
c) Whitewater rafting
d) Hang gliding

6. If Zac could have any original copy of a classic novel, what would it be?

a) *The Lord of the Rings*
b) *Animal Farm*
c) *Robinson Crusoe*
d) *Lord of the Flies*

7. For another present you get him a DVD, but what film would he prefer?

a) *Lords of Dogtown*
b) *Harry Potter and the Order of the Phoenix*
c) *I Am Legend*
d) *Juno*

8. If Zac could have any original comic book, what would it be?

a) *Superman*
b) *X-Men*
c) *Spiderman*
d) *Batman*

9. Zac always likes to spend his birthday with his family, but how many siblings does he have?

a) One sister
b) Two brothers
c) One brother
d) One brother and one sister

10. At the end of the big day, Zac wants to curl up on the sofa and watch some TV. Which programme would he most like to watch?

a) *Big Brother*
b) *Gossip Girl*
c) *One Tree Hill*
d) *American Idol*

How did you score? Did you get enough points to hang out with Zac on his big day?

0-2 – You need to learn more about Zac if you're going to make him feel special on his birthday.

3-5 – Not bad, Zac might make time for a quick coffee with you on his special day.

6-8 – You sure know your stuff! You get an invite to Zac's birthday party.

9+ – Lucky you! You get to spend the whole day with the birthday boy!

Answers on P.61

INTERESTS AND HOBBIES

RUN, ZAC, RUN!

No matter where he is in the world, Zac has to start every morning with a run. He loves to plug in his iPod and run along his local stretch of sand, Manhattan Beach in LA. He's a complete fitness addict, which explains his healthy, toned look. And it's all thanks to Sylvester Stallone. 'After watching the entire *Rocky* series, I got hooked on fitness,' says Zac. He now has the *Rocky* theme tune as the ringtone on his mobile phone.

Now he's an A-list star, there's no room for complacency and he has to make sure he's in good shape at all times. A major reason directors and producers of films such as *Hairspray* and *HSM* are so keen to sign him up is his ability to run through dance routines for 12 hours at a time. It's not all about having a winning smile and a cute haircut. Films, and especially musicals, are an endurance test for the body and he's got to make sure he's physically ready at all times.

SPORTS

One of the greatest differences between Zac and Troy is Zac's inability to play sports well. 'When I was younger I tried the whole "little league" thing. I tried baseball; I was bad at it. I tried basketball; I was bad at it. That might be one of the reasons I got into acting. Nowadays, I don't do any real conventional sports, sometimes though you might find me

Zac Fact

If Zac could get any celebrity's autograph it would be Kobe Bryant's.

in the yard shooting hoops or playing hacky sack.' Ever modest about his talents, Zac says: 'I was the worst kid on my sixth-grade basketball team. I passed the ball to the wrong team and they scored at the buzzer in double overtime to win the championship. It's one of those memories that still makes you squirm when you think about it.'

These days, when it comes to team sports, Zac is more an observer than a participator. His favourite baseball team is the San Francisco Giants, and his favourite player is Barry Bonds – he even has a signed baseball that Jay Leno gave him.

As a young teenager Zac got into adrenaline sports like skiing, snowboarding and rock climbing, but his main passion was skateboarding. He says: 'One day I'd love to do a skydive. I'm definitely going to do it in the next year.' Also, just like Troy in *HSM 2*, Zac is a keen golfer and often makes it out to LA's courses for a swift 18 holes. Ever since filming *The Derby Stallion*, he's had an interest in horses, and loves to take a steed out for a gallop along the Malibu beaches whenever he gets a chance.

✺ SURF'S UP!

Playing the role of sultry surfer Cameron Bale in teen drama *Summerland* sparked Zac's interest in surfing, and he got his first surfboard and wet suit from his parents the Christmas after he started filming the show. Out in the water, next to all the fiercely territorial surfers, Zac was literally out of his depth. 'I got crushed by a wave and held under the water for about ten seconds. It was pretty scary.' However, after a while he picked it up and is pretty good at it: 'I'm hitting the waves all over the place.' But isn't he scared of shark attacks? 'In San Luis Obispo we've had a couple of shark sightings, but so what? Here's the thing – if a shark bites you, you are the luckiest dude in the world because you are a legend forever.' If you say so, Zac!

Zac on playing basketball in the *HSM* auditions: 'We had to play basketball,' he says. 'I was probably the weakest at that.' Luckily his singing and dancing were good enough that he made it through.

FOX

teen Choice '07

FOX

teen CHOIC '07

teen

teen

ZAC'S FAVOURITE ALBUM RELEASES IN 2008

Radiohead
In Rainbows

 Madonna
Hard Candy

Alanis Morissette
Flavours of Entanglement

Coldplay
Viva la Vida

The Von Bondies
We are Kamikazes

✸ MUSIC

Zac has had music running through his veins ever since he could talk. 'I've always been singing. Since day one,' says Zac. But despite having chart-topping success with 'Get'cha Head in the Game' and 'Breaking Free', Zac is keen to focus on acting, for now. 'I'm going to work primarily on the acting, to try to make a foundation for myself for the future … I'm definitely just an actor.' Even big money deals from the likes of Simon Cowell (of *X Factor* fame) have been turned down in favour of concentrating on his acting. 'I'm trying to steer clear of the whole music thing at this point. I think the most important thing is to establish myself as an actor. I think it's very easy for people to start getting confused when they see a CD come out.'

Unfortunately, it looks as if we won't be seeing a Zac album launch in the near future, but that's not to say he's not always plugged into his iPod: 'I'm into anything and everything. I'll just go onto iTunes and download hundreds of things.'

ZAC'S TOP FIVE IPOD PLAYLISTS

Party List

Kings of Leon – 'King of the Rodeo'
Gym Class Heroes – 'Cupid's Chokehold'
Justin Timberlake – 'Rock Your Body'
Kanye West – 'Stronger'
Mark Ronson – 'Ooh Wee'

On-The-Go

Yeah Yeah Yeahs – 'Gold Lion'
Lenny Kravitz – 'Fly Away'
The Postal Service – 'Such Great Heig
Vampire Weekend – 'Mansard Roof'
Modest Mouse – 'The World at Large'

Chilling

Jack Johnson – 'Better Together'
John Mayer – 'Waiting on the World to Change'
Coldplay – 'Violet Hill'
Cat Power – 'Sea of Love'
Xavier Rudd – 'Let Me Be'

SUDOKU

Fill in the boxes so each one contains a drawing of Troy, Gabriella, Sharpay, Chad, Ryan and Monique. Don't forget, every row across and column down must contain all six pictures, so use a pencil before using a pen just in case you make a mistake!

Answers on page 61

50

ZAC WORD SEARCH

Search for the words listed below in the grid. The words can run horizontally, diagonally or from top to bottom.

```
E U O P C X T R U K A R S O P C X
T U U K M C R F A W I L D C A T S V
A T I N L G M X N N B B R I A I N O
H I E Q Y U Z F I P B O D L M E A E
O E S N M I L R T N J E U E Q J P A
R S W U S R O A F O N D K Q O Y I I
U W C G I D Y B E N J E U A L R T T
T Z F X A B R I E L L A K L R M P V
Y C T T U C O R B I N B R A V
P F S N G I F U N I K I E R A W
A S H L E Y U S H V F Z N A B N M A
R O A P O D E H A Y E E Y I E L C R
D V F T N G R N E B U Z A A R U S O
O H U K A R P A S B J Q E X A Y C X
T D V F T S N G U F U N B R A I N R
```

ZAC   WILDCATS
RYAN   SHARPAY
TROY   VANESSA
TAYLOR   ASHLEY
GABRIELLA   CORBIN

Answers on page 61

ZAC CROSSWORD

ACROSS
1. The number of dogs Zac owns (3)
3. Zac's character's surname in *HSM* (6)
5. A TV hospital drama Zac had a cameo in (2)
6. The first name of the actor that plays Chad (6)
7. Zac's latest hit film that's also a number (9)
9. Ashley Tisdale's character in *HSM* (7)
11. Zac's home state (10)
12. Zac and Vanessa's joint name (7)

DOWN
2. Troy's basketball team in HSM (8)
4. The surname of Zac's hero and co-star in Hairspray (8)
7. A TV show Zac starred in with Lori Loughlan (10)
8. Vanessa's character in *HSM* (9)
10. The hit film Zac's co-star John Travolta made his name in (6)

FORTUNE TELLER

Make your very own fortune teller to find out what your and Zac's destiny holds.

Fill your Zac fortune teller with great predictions such as ...

You're ZAC's TRUE LOVE
ZAC AND VANESSA FOREVER
You're ZAC'S BEST PAL FOREVER
ZAC IS, LIKE, SO OVER YOU

YOU WILL NEED:

★ A square piece of paper
★ Pens
★ Pencils

INSTRUCTIONS:

1. Find the middle of the paper by folding it from corner to corner.

2. Fold each corner to the centre to make a smaller square.

3. Turn the square over, and turn each corner to the centre again to make an even smaller square.

4. Turn over again. Draw a different colour on each quarter of the square.

5. Turn over again. Put numbers 1 to 8 on each segment.

6. Open out each flap and write a message behind each number.

7. Put the thumb and forefinger of each hand into a segment and close up the fortune teller. First ask your pal to choose a colour. If they choose BLUE, spell out B-L-U-E and open and shut the fortune teller four times. Then ask your pal to choose a number from the four numbers showing. Open and shut the fortune teller the same number of times. Then, ask them to choose another number, open up the flap and read them the message hidden underneath.

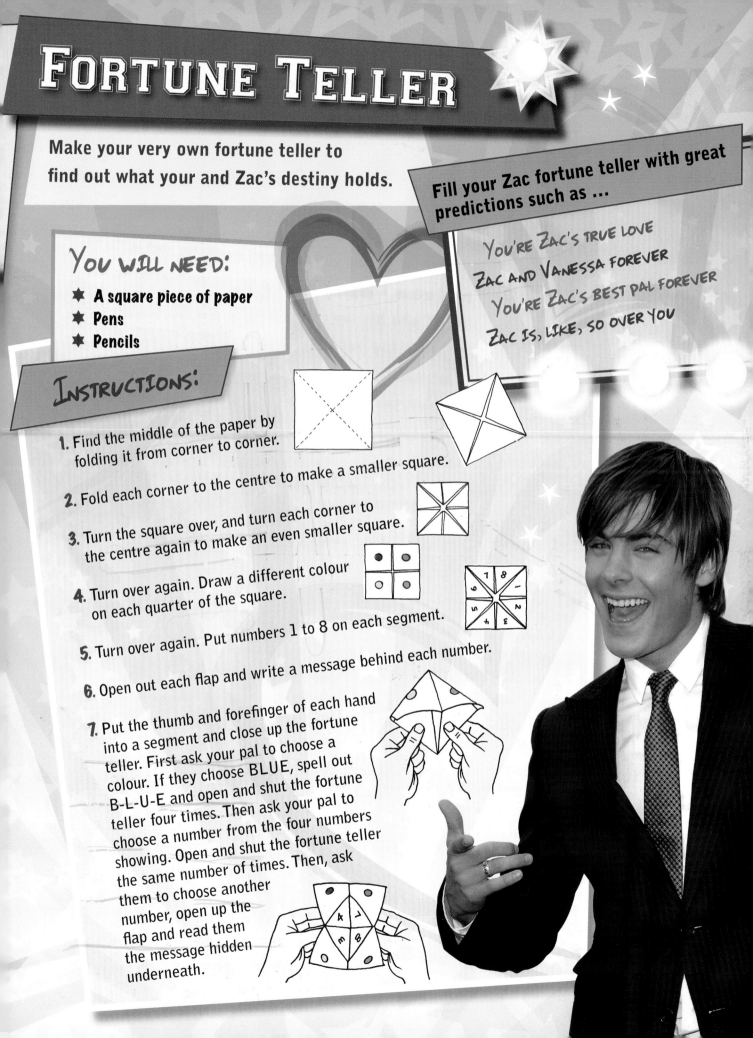

Zac's Top
BURGER N' SHAKE
Recipe

Zac loves nothing more than hanging out with his pals while slurping down a shake and sinking his teeth into his favourite burger. So, we've got hold of Zac's top-secret burger 'n' shake recipe so you can really impress him when he comes for dinner! Remember, ask your parents for help with the hot stuff (frying and grilling) and the milkshake blending.

YOU WILL NEED:

For the Burger
* Beef mincemeat (allow 4oz/110g per person) and one egg yolk (or you can use pre-made burgers from the fridge/freezer)
* Burger buns – one per burger
* Cheese slices – as many as you like!
* 2-3 gherkins or pickles
* Mustard
* Mayonnaise
* Tomato ketchup
* 1 small red onion
* Slices of tomato
* Lettuce leaves

INSTRUCTIONS:

For the Shake
* Ice cream (any flavour will do, but Zac likes chocolate, of course!)
* Milk
* Optional coloured sprinkles, marshmallows or edible glitter

TO MAKE THE BURGER:

1. If you are using pre-made burgers, follow the manufacturer's cooking instructions. If you are making your own – and it's a lot of fun – put the mincemeat and egg yolk into a large bowl and, using washed hands, mix them together. Don't be afraid to get really stuck in and thoroughly squeeze the mincemeat in with the egg. Gooey! Separate the mixture into even portions and shape the meat into burger patties.

2. Grab your parents and ask them to fry your burgers for you in a little olive oil or even better, ask them to fire up the barbeque and cook them on that – Zac's favourite!

3. While the burgers are turning golden brown, pop the burger buns under a hot grill for just a few minutes each side – do keep an eye on them as Zac doesn't like burnt buns and be very careful of the heat. Even better, ask your parents to do this for you.

4. When the buns are golden brown, using a spatula or oven gloves, carefully take them off the grill. Spread a thin layer of English mustard onto the bottom bun, followed by a layer of mayo and a thick layer of tomato ketchup. Of course, if you don't like any of these you can add your own sauces or leave the buns plain. But Zac loves them all!

5. Wash the lettuce and tomatoes, and ask your parents to chop the gherkins, red onions and tomatoes into thin slices. You can have them all lined up on the chopping board ready to load into a delicious high stack!

6. Place the burgers onto the bottom bun (and that oozing ketchup) and add a cheese slice onto the meat. Then go crazy and pile up your favourite toppings. Add as much as you like and don't forget – Zac likes plenty of lettuce, cheese, red onions, gherkins, tomatoes and a big squirt of ketchup to top it all off. Delicious!

TO MAKE THE SHAKE:

1. Choose your favourite flavour of ice cream, but remember Zac's favourite is chocolate.

2. Scoop out three spoons of ice cream into a blender. Measure out half a cup of milk and pour it in.

3. Make sure the lid of the blender is closed securely – get your parents to check this before you start as you don't want milkshake sprayed all over the kitchen! Blend the milk and ice cream together until smooth.

4. Pour the milkshake into a glass. Add some coloured sprinkles or edible glitter or floating marshmallows on top and stick in a big straw. Now you are free to glug away, but don't get brain freeze!

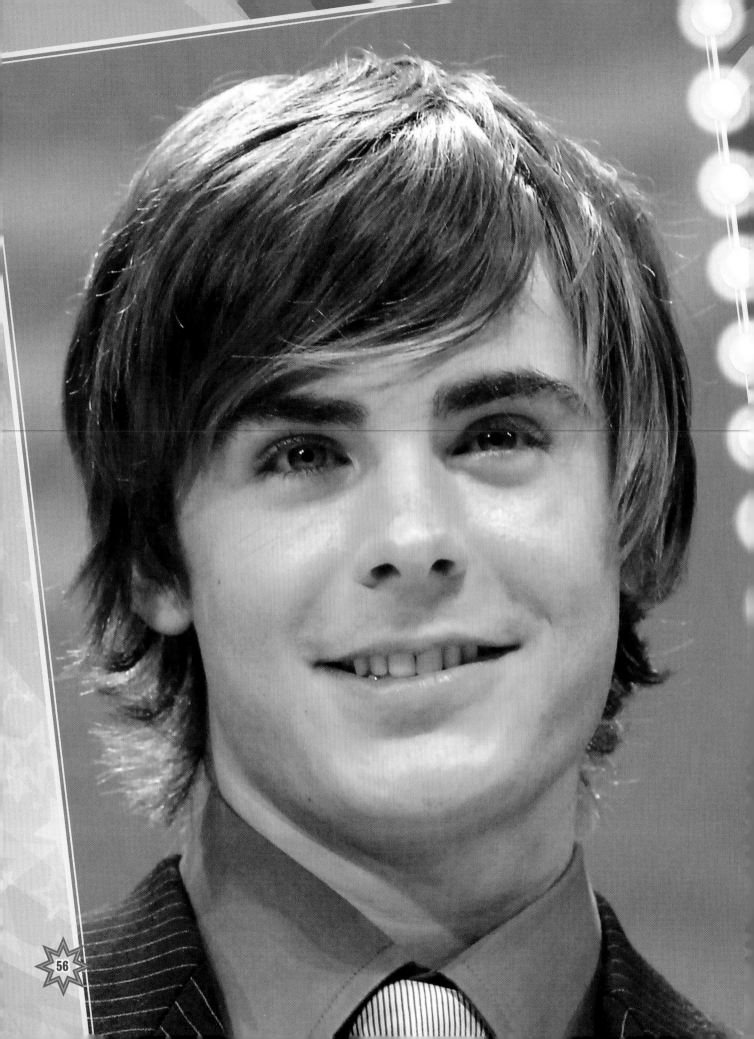

Looking At The STARS

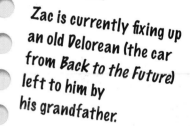

ZAC'S LIKES

✓ Getting notes and emails
✓ Being pampered
✓ Pretty trinkets
✓ Praise

ZAC'S ASTROLOGY

Just like Troy, Zac's sign, libra, means he's excellent in friendships and partnerships, meaning he plays well with a team, such as the Wildcats. His charm and co-operative nature makes him a great person to smooth over rough spots when friends have a disagreement. He is a faithful and honest friend and they trust him with their deepest secrets. He is also very artistic and loves drawing, painting, singing and acting, of course.

He has a hard time making decisions and can be torn between two passions – like music and acting, perhaps? Sometimes he is afraid of making the wrong choice, so he mopes around and worries about it much longer than he should. He also gets cranky when he is forced to make up his mind before he's ready! So no pressure on him, girls!

ZAC'S DISLIKES

✗ Shouting
✗ Slopiness
✗ Dirty places
✗ Critisism

FAMILY

Zac's family will play a significant part in his life in 2009, as his increasing work commitments will make him realise how important it is to have a supportive home environment. Sure, a younger brother can still be annoying, but where his pranks might have upset him last year, they'll make Zac laugh in 2009 as his mood will be sky high!

LOVE

Romance does very well this year. With existing relationships taking on new levels of commitment and trust, there's a possibility of maybe moving in with his partner or finding a new partner altogether. So does this spell the end for 'Zanessa' or the start of exciting things for the couple?

FRIENDSHIP

This is the year for talking, with Zac giving and receiving plenty of advice from those close to him, especially his Taurean, Libran, Cancerian (Ashley Tisdale) and Virgoan pals. He should show emotional awareness around March, which is Oscar season, when his pals will need him the most.

CAREER

Big opportunities and hefty responsibilities may arise. He shouldn't back out from an opportunity in September simply because it may appear like a lot of work. He should also try something new. So more films and great success loom for Zac in 2009, but maybe this will push him out of his song-and-dance comfort zone. Expect to see a more serious and mature Zac in the coming year.

Zac Fact

- Zac's duet with Vanessa, 'Breaking Free', made the fastest climb in American chart history – climbing from number 86 to 4 in only 14 days.

Looking To The Future

Despite talk that *HSM 4* has already been written, it's safe to say that *HSM 3* was Zac's last outing as a Troy Bolton. He's now looking ahead to bigger and better things to further his career. The young star is being pretty coy about any future projects that may be in the pipeline, but the rumour mill has suggested that in 2009 he may do a remake of Kevin Bacon's *Footloose* or even star in a life-story of Andy Warhol.

One thing's for sure – we won't see Zac waste his talent by hitting the wild celebrity-party circuit. 'I don't find myself drawn to that scene,' says Zac. 'I think acting is a tradition that far predates celebrity and, today, the two are just meshing. It's not even that I've made a conscious decision not to party. I don't think clubbing is a choice you make. You can have fun with friends without being part of that scene.'

So 2009 is looking bright for our *High School Musical* heart-throb. But will happen in 2010 and beyond? Watch this space to find out …

Zac was born on 18 October 1987

Other famous Librans include Gwen Stefani, John Lennon, Matt Damon, Sting, Mahatma Ghandi, Avril Lavigne, NSYNC's Chris Kirkpatrick and Gwyneth Paltrow.

Zac Is Most Compatible With

- ♥ **Aquarius** – a marvellous match
- ♥ **Gemini** – sublime
- ♥ **Aries** – opposites attract
- ♥ **Scorpio** – emotionally rewarding
- ♥ **Taurus** – very sensual

Zac Is Least Compatible With

- ✗ **Capricorn** – don't bet on this one
- ✗ **Cancer** – very hard work
- ✗ **Virgo** – discordant
- ✗ **Libra** – indecisive!
- ✗ **Sagittarius** (Vanessa Hudgens) – too flighty

ANSWERS

THE ZAC QUIZ P 14

1. **c)** David and Alexander
2. **b)** Libra
3. **c)** *Summerland*
4. **b)** Dylan
5. **d)** John Mayer
6. **c)** San Luis Obispo
7. **c)** Liger (the lion and tiger mix-breed)
8. **a)** *The Goonies*
9. **b)** Peter Parker
10. **a)** Hollywood
11. **d)** Simon
12. **d)** *Rocco's Modern Life*
13. **c)** Sushi
14. **a)** Toyota Supra
15. **b)** Humming
16. **c)** Kobe Bryant
17. **a)** *Rocky*
18. **b)** Jessica Alba
19. **d)** London
20. **c)** A run

ZAC BIRTHDAY QUIZ P 42

1. **b)** 18 October
2. **a)** Granola
3. **c)** Postal Service
4. **c)** Cherry Garcia
5. **a)** Skydiving
6. **c)** *Robinson Crusoe*
7. **a)** *Lords of Dogtown*
8. **c)** *Spiderman*
9. **c)** One brother
10. **d)** *American Idol*

SUDOKU P 50

ZAC CROSSWORD P 54

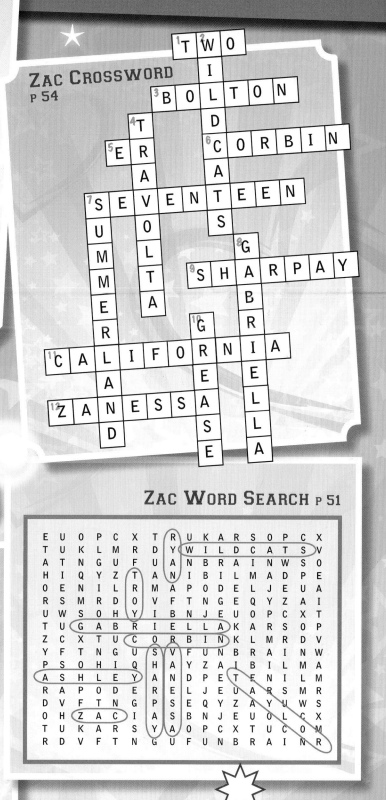

ZAC WORD SEARCH P 51

First published in hardback in Great Britain in 2008 by
Orion Books
an imprint of the Orion Publishing Group Ltd
Orion House, 5 Upper St Martin's Lane,
London WC2H 9EA
An Hachette Livre UK Company

1 3 5 7 9 10 8 6 4 2

A CIP catalogue record for this book is available
from the British Library.

ISBN: 978 1 4091 0063 8

Printed in Italy by Rotolito Lombarda

The Orion Publishing Group's policy is to use papers that are natural, renewable
and recyclable and made from wood grown in sustainable forests. The logging and
manufacturing processes are expected to conform to the environmental regulations
of the country of origin.

Every effort has been made to fulfil requirements with regard to reproducing copyright
material. The author and publisher will be glad to rectify any omissions at the earliest
opportunity.

www.orionbooks.co.uk

Picture Credits

GETTY IMAGES: 4, 5, 6, 9, 12, 13, 16 (left), 18, 19, 21(left), 22 (right), 23 (left),
30 (bottom left), 32, 38, 39, 40, 45, 48, 49, 50 (top left) 52 (left and top right),
53, 54 (top left) 56, 60, 63
REX FEATURES: 2, 3 (top and bottom right), 7, 8, 13, 14, 16 (right), 17, 22 (left),
23 (right), 25 (centre), 28, 30 (bottom), 31, 33, 35, 41 (top and bottom), 43, 44, 50
(left centre), 52 (top left), 54 (bottom right), 57
PA PHOTOS: 11, 20, 21 (right), 24, 25 (right) 26, 29, 30 (top and bottom right),
33, 34, 36, 37, 41 (right), 46, 47 (top), 50 (bottom left and right), 52 (bottom right),
54 (right), 58
CORBIS PHOTOS: 10, 15, 47 (bottom), 51, 59